An Intimate Note
to the Sincere Seeker

SRI SRI
RAVI SHANKAR

VOLUME 3: JUNE 18, 1997—JULY 23, 1998

ART OF LIVING FOUNDATION

AN INTIMATE NOTE TO THE SINCERE SEEKER
Weekly Knowledge from Sri Sri Ravi Shankar
Volume 3: June 18, 1997—July 23, 1998

Compiled by David L. Burge

©Copyright 1998 by Art of Living Foundation
All rights reserved.

Art of Living Foundation
P.O. Box 50003
Santa Barbara, California 93150
Telephone: (805) 563-6396
Books and Tapes: (800) 574-3001

David L. Gary Bill Anne
Burge Boucherle Hayden Elixhauser

Design, Type, Editing, and Production by David L. Burge and team: Gary Boucherle, Noelle Parnell, Laura Weinberg, Ceci Balmer, and Richard Burge, with special Editorial Assistance from Mary Hunter Leach and Janael McQueen.

Weekly Knowledge Coordinators: Bill Hayden and Anne Elixhauser

Sudarshan Kriya and *Sahaj Samadhi Meditation* are service marks of the Art of Living Foundation, a nonprofit educational organization.

*H*ere in your hands is
the third treasure book
of intimate notes from
Sri Sri Ravi Shankar
—*a gift of love to cherish.*

Contents

- 106 Sensitivity and Strength 7
- 107 The Personal and the Impersonal 9
- 108 The Golden Veil 11
- 109 With Whom Are You At Ease 13
- 110 Let Love Be 15
- 111 Make Everything Personal & Universal 16
- 112 On Respect 18
- 113 Sacrifice 20
- 114 Window Shutters 22
- 115 Raksha Bandhan 23
- 116 Truth Once Found 25
- 117 A Big Dilemma 27
- 118 How to Get Centered 29
- 119 The Five Insights 30
- 120 Five Signs of the Satguru 32
- 121 Six Signs of a Seeker 34
- 122 Yagyas 36
- 123 God as a Child 37
- 124 Feel Blessed 39
- 125 Diwali 41
- 126 Love is Your Very Existence 43
- 127 Your Expressions of Love 45
- 128 Ego 47
- 129 Memory 49
- 130 Intellect 51
- 131 Time and Mind 53
- 132 Faces of Infinity 55
- 133 Celebration and the Christmas Tree 56
- 134 A Wise Person is Happy Even in Bad Times 58
- 135 You are Pure Electricity 60

136	Politics 62	150	Do Not Follow Me 88
137	Tolerance and Acceptance are Not Virtues 64	151	Confusion and Decision 90
		152	You are Privileged 92
138	False Security 66	153	The Value of Chanting 94
139	Organization and Devotion 68	154	Intensify Your Longing 96
140	When a Mistake is Not a Mistake 70	155	Faith is Your Wealth 98
		156	Who Wakes Up First? 101
141	Respect 72	157	Breaking Beyond the Rational Mind 103
142	Shiva and Vashi 74		
143	Formality and Cordiality 76	158	If You Cannot Meditate—Be Stupid! 105
144	You are the Tenth 78	159	Give Away Your Rights 107
145	Inside Out 80		
146	Dreams 82	160	Generosity is a Quality of Spirit 109
147	Impression and Expression 83		
		161	The Path of Love is Surrender 111
148	Tarka, Vitarka, and Kutarka 85		
		162	It Takes Courage to Say "I Am" 113
149	Softness and Forcefulness 87		
		163	Do You Know I Have No Mercy? 115

The Art of Living Foundation 117

Since June, 1995, people around the world eagerly await the Weekly Knowledge from Sri Sri. It started out as a simple note from the Master. Later, devotees began to add a weekly "News Flash" to capture a feeling of the events surrounding Sri Sri on his extensive travels.

Different people from various countries assist the Master with transcribing, translating, and transmitting the Weekly Knowledge. Next week it could be you!

This collection contains Volume 3, Weekly Knowledge from June 18, 1997 through July 23, 1998.

June 18, 1997
Montreal Ashram, Canada

106 Sensitivity and Strength

Those who are sensitive often feel weak. Those who feel strong are often insensitive.

Some people are sensitive to themselves but insensitive to others. They often feel the others are the "bad guys."

Those who are sensitive to others but not to themselves often end up feeling *Poor me.*

Some conclude it's better not to be sensitive, because sensitivity brings pain. They shut off. But mind you, if you are not sensitive, you will lose all the finer things in life, too—intuition, beauty, and ecstasy of love.

Insensitive people usually do not recognize their weakness. And those who are sensitive do not recognize that their sensitivity is their strength.

This path and this Knowledge make you strong and sensitive.

Sensitivity is intuition. Sensitivity is compassion. Sensitivity is love. Sensitivity is the real strength: calmness, endurance, silence, non-reactiveness, confidence, faith—and a smile.

Be both sensitive and strong.

✏️ **News Flash**

From India: The children at the ashram school have the best test scores in the entire district, and the enrollment has doubled to four hundred and fifty.

Exercise:

In your own Satsang group, see how both sensitivity and strength have grown.

June 25, 1997
Montreal Ashram, Canada

107 The Personal and the Impersonal

WHEN YOU LOVE SOMETHING, IT BECOMES ALIVE. With love, the whole creation becomes personal.

For children, everything is personal. Children make each toy come alive. Even a tree has a face, even the sun laughs, and even a stone attracts reverence when it becomes personal.

Susannah: Yes! In a temple even a stone is elevated to the level of spirit.

Sri Sri: In love, you raise even objects to life. If you remove love, even people become objects.

Violence is removing love. How could a person kill another? Only when they see them as an object, not as a person.

Dean: The military trains soldiers to see people as objects.

Sri Sri: People who see God as impersonal do not progress. The impersonal cannot attract your love or reverence.

Dean and Susannah: That's why we need a Guru!

Chan: When we personalize something, we make it real. So then, what is reality?

Sri Sri: YOU are the Reality. You are not the thoughts, you are not the emotions—nor the actions. You are not even a person…!

✎ News Flash

The Weekly Knowledge books for the first two years are being released by David and Gary. In a debate about whether or not to include the News Flashes, the majority voted in favor.

Every day Guruji continues to be inundated with letters that report amazing healing experiences.

Art of Living Teachers in North America are now observing two weeks of intense Sadhana.

Advanced Courses are happening in Poona, Slovenia, Botswana and Montreal.

People are enjoying a totally different side of Guruji this week with his fiery talks that have made everyone sit up and take notice.

Exercise:

What you now see as impersonal, see as personal. And when you feel any negative emotion towards anybody, see that person as impersonal—pretend that you are a robot.

July 2, 1997
Montreal Ashram, Canada

108 The Golden Veil

CRAVING COMES FROM ENCOURAGING THE THOUGHT of pleasure.

Georgia: That's why we spend so much time in our minds!

Whether you encourage a worldly thought or a Divine thought, they both bring you pleasure. Worldly thoughts lead you from pleasure down to indulgence, disappointment and dejection. Divine thoughts take you from pleasure up to bliss, intelligence, and progress in life.

A worldly thought brings pleasure as memory, yet the actual experience of that pleasure may not be as great as the memory. A Divine thought materializes as Reality.

Question: What is a Divine thought?

Sri Sri: "I am not the body; I am bliss, satchitananda; I am unbounded space; I am love; I am peace; I am light."

Question: What is a worldly thought?

Sri Sri: It is a thought about money, sex, food, power, status and self-image.

Truth is hidden by the golden veil of the mundane. Pierce through this glittering sheath and know you are the Sun.

In the world, everybody is after GOLD; some are after GOOD; only a few are after GOD.

Transcend GOLD, transcend the GOOD, and reach GOD.

✎ News Flash

As Advanced Course participants move from the small mind to the Big Mind, the children move super-sized frogs from the small pond to the big lake. Both frogs and humans are happy in their spacious abodes. The ART Excel* course is a big hit with the young people.

Vasishta makes regular visits each noontime, as we read his ancient teachings in the Yogavasishta.

*All-'Round Training for Excellence—Sri Sri's program for youths

July 9, 1997
Montreal Ashram, Canada

109 With Whom Are You At Ease?

WITH WHOM DO YOU FEEL REALLY COMFORTABLE and at ease?

With someone who does not question your love, someone who takes for granted that you love them. Isn't it?

When someone doubts your love and you constantly have to prove it, this becomes a heavy load on your head. They start questioning you and demanding explanations for all your actions. To explain everything you do is a burden. Your nature is to shed the burden because you don't feel comfortable.

When you question the reason behind someone's action, you are asking for justice for yourself. You create a distance when you ask for justice. Your whole intention is to come close, but instead you create a distance.

You are the Eternal Witness. You are as much a witness to your own actions as you are to someone else's. When someone asks you for an explanation for your actions, they are speaking from doership and imposing that doership on you. This brings you discomfort.

Neither demand an explanation, nor give an explanation.

If somebody is just there with you, like a part of you,

they don't question you. They are like your arm. There is a closeness and unity that goes beyond all demands and questions.

✎ News Flash

The big frogs have hopped back to the small pond!

Pitaji* has arrived in North America for the first time and we are enjoying his stories from the Puranas.

A well-known acupuncturist from China, Dr. Sha, came to take Guruji's blessings.

The question basket is bringing forth extraordinarily deep and beautiful knowledge.

*Sri Sri's father

July 16, 1997
Topanga Canyon, California

110 Let Love Be

*L*ET LOVE BE. DON'T GIVE LOVE A NAME. WHEN YOU give love a name, it becomes a relationship, and relationship restricts love.

There is love between you and me. Just let it be. If you name love as brother, sister, mother, father, Guru, you are making it into a relationship. Relationship restricts love.

What is your relationship to yourself? Are you your wife, brother, husband, Guru?

Let love be. Don't give it a name.

✍ News Flash

At the end of the Montreal Advanced Course, Guruji went for a swim. From underneath a waterfall, he beckoned, "If the course didn't help you become silent, then come sit under the waterfall."

The party moved on to the Agape Church in California where there was joyous singing of "Hoya Heya."

The phone is ringing off the hook as people from all over the world prepare to gather at Lake Tahoe for Guru Purnima.

July 23, 1997
Tahoe City, California

111 Make Everything Personal and Universal

Manatha Sri Jaganatha
Madguru Sri Jagadguru
Madathma Sarva Bhutatma
Tasmai Sri Gurave Namah

My Lord, Lord of Creation
My Master, Master of the universe
My soul, soul of all living beings
To him, my gloriously radiant Master, I bow down

*O*FTEN WHAT IS UNIVERSAL WE DO NOT CONSIDER as personal, and what is personal we do not consider as belonging to everyone. What is "mine" and what is "universal" are found completely opposite. This causes greed, fear, jealousy, and lack of contentment.

On this Guru Purnima, wake up and realize that the Lord of the universe is very personal to you. Your personal Master is the Lord of the whole world. The Master is your very Self, and your Self is the very life in every being.

Make the universal personal and you become richer, wiser, stronger.

Make the personal universal and you will find freedom, compassion, love.

📣 News Flash

The Guru Purnima explosion of bliss is still going on for six hundred course participants at Lake Tahoe and for devotees around the world. Guruji continues to thrill us with singing, laughter, knowledge, and new meditations. Everyone and everything is sky high here—altitude, attitude, consciousness, cake, and water balloons. Many Centers around the world celebrated Guru Purnima by starting seva projects in their areas.

July 30, 1997
German Academy

112 On Respect

Question: What do you do if people don't respect you?

Sri Sri: Thank them. They have given you freedom. *[laughter and amazement]*

When people respect you, they often take away your freedom. They expect you to smile at them, recognize them, behave in a certain way with them.

When people don't respect you, you are not obliged to answer their questions and you can drop all formalities. You can naturally smile or frown—you can be complete.

When people love and respect you, you are obliged to return their courtesies because you don't want to hurt them. When they don't respect or love you, they will not be hurt by your expressions. They set you free.

You often gain respect at the cost of your freedom. Wisdom is to put the freedom first and not bother about respect.

Question: Won't freedom bring arrogance?

Sri Sri: True freedom is not an "I don't care" attitude; it is not stiff. It is an inner lightness with a genuine smile. When someone is stiff and arrogant, they are not free. Love blossoms only in freedom.

When there is love, respect simply follows you.

✍ **News Flash**

Midway through the ART Excel Course at Lake Tahoe, the teenagers staged a "rebellion" against their course teachers. All problems dissolved as everyone sat in Guruji's presence.

The American tour ended with an outdoor Satsang at Emerald Bay overlooking Lake Tahoe.

Now on to the European summer celebrations...

August 6, 1997
German Academy

113 Sacrifice

Sacrifice is letting go of something you are holding onto—something you are attached to which gives you pleasure—for something bigger that would bring good.

Sacrifice brings strength in life. Life without sacrifice is stagnant. Sacrifice gives you a quantum leap to a higher pedestal.

Often people think sacrifice makes life dull and joyless. In fact, it is sacrifice that makes life worth living. The amount of sacrifice in your life brings out your magnanimity and helps you move out of misery.

A life without sacrifice is worth nothing. Zeal, enthusiasm, strength and joy are all connected to sacrifice.

Question: Some people say, "I have sacrificed so much," and complain.

Sri Sri: That is good. The thought of sacrifice has given them strength—to complain! This saves them from blaming themselves, otherwise they would be more depressed.

Sacrifice never goes unrewarded. There can be no love, no wisdom, no true joy without sacrifice.

Sacrifice makes you sacred.

Become sacred!

News Flash

A team of three Art of Living teachers went to facilitate the peace process between Armenia and Azerbaidzhan in Karabakh, conducting three courses for Army officials and another series for civilians. An article in the Moscow Times reported that the factions had agreed to stop fighting only two weeks after our team started work there.

From the German Academy: Imagine translations in ten languages simultaneously! Yet the course participants all speak one language—silence.

August 13, 1997
Stockholm, Sweden

114 Window Shutters

To the degree that you are awake, everything around you brings knowledge. If you are not awake, even the most precious knowledge does not make any sense.

(Suddenly there was much noise from outside and Kiran went to shut the window.)

Awareness depends upon your ability to open and shut your windows. When there is a storm, you need to shut your windows—otherwise you will get wet. When it is hot and suffocating inside, you need to open your windows.

Your senses are like windows. When you are awake, you have the ability to open and shut your windows at will; then you are free.

If your windows cannot be shut or opened at will, you are bound. Attending to this is sadhana, or spiritual practice.

✍ News Flash

In Copenhagen, Sri Sri was featured on "Good Morning Denmark."

Extensive media coverage of Sri Sri's visit to Stockholm brought far more people for the evening program than could be accommodated. Guruji first greeted those who could not get in—the last shall be first!

August 20, 1997
Denmark

115 Raksha Bandhan

Today's full moon is dedicated to the seers—the rishis. It is called the *raksha bandhan*.

Bandhan means bondage; *raksha* means protection—a bondage that protects you.

Your bondage to the Knowledge, to the Master, to the Truth, to the Self—all saves you.

A rope can be tied to protect you or to strangle you. The small mind with mundane things can strangle you. The Big Mind, the Knowledge, saves you.

Your bondage to the Master, to the Truth, to the ancient Knowledge of the rishis—is your savior.

Raksha bandhan is the bondage that saves you. You are saved by your bondage to the Satsang.

Bondage is essential in life. Only let the bondage be to the Divine—in a life free from bondage.

Question: Who is an atheist?
Sri Sri: One who has a concept of God.

Question: What is peace?
Sri Sri: Undivided mind.

✎ News Flash

Oslo, Norway: In the same hall where the Nobel Peace Prize is awarded, Guruji's evening meditation brought priceless peace.

Arhus, Denmark: The Advanced Course hall was hot and humid and the speaker system did not work, but everyone dissolved into profound knowledge.

TV stations interviewed Guruji, and several newspapers carried articles in Scandinavia.

August 27, 1997
German Academy

116 Truth Once Found

THE INTELLECT DIVIDES AND SYNTHESIZES.
Some creatures in the world synthesize and some creatures divide. But a human being has both abilities.

Ants synthesize; they build an anthill and collect things together. A beaver synthesizes by bringing wood together to build a dam. Birds also synthesize (such as the weaver birds).

Monkeys cannot synthesize, they divide everything. Give them a garland and they will tear it to pieces and throw it all over the place! A monkey can only divide and analyze.

A human being both divides (analyzes) and synthesizes. The intellect analyzes the relative world to find the Truth. And Truth once found synthesizes everything into One.

When the intellect becomes quiet, it brings out intelligence. Usually people think that gathering information makes one intelligent. This is not so. It is *samadhi* that brings intelligence.

An unintelligent man, though he may have all the information, cannot be creative. An intelligent man, even without much information, can be creative.

A sign of intelligence is to see the One in many and find the many in One.

There is an old Sanskrit proverb:

The first sign of intelligence is not to start anything.

The second sign of intelligence is: if you have started something, you have to continue it to the end.

So, if you have annoyed somebody, don't stop it in the middle, take him to the edge! *(laughter)*

🖊 News Flash

Bellund, Denmark: One-hundred-fifty Advanced Course participants enjoyed good silence, meditations, and lively Satsangs with interesting questions and answers, tears of gratitude, and lots of laughter.

Sri Sri's "secret" excursion to the beach had 50 devotees trailing behind. A driver became so blissed out in Guruji's presence that he drove the fun-train off the normal beach track into main road traffic—to the amazement of the onlooking citizens.

With less than two weeks of preparation, the Hamburg devotees had a full hall for Sri Sri's talk.

This week also included an Advanced Course in Calcutta, big Satsangs in Durban, Krishna's birthday celebrations at the German Academy, and Teacher Training at the Bangalore Ashram.

September 3, 1997
Mumbai, India

117 A Big Dilemma

*I*f you have complete faith, there are no questions. If you have no faith, there is no point in asking, because how will you have faith in the answer?

Harish: What about the questions we ask you with complete faith?

Sri Sri: If you have faith in God, when you know somebody is taking care of you, then what is the need to ask any question? If you have taken the Karnataka Express to Bangalore, is there a need to ask at every station, "Where is the train going?"

And when you have someone who is looking after your desires, then why go to an astrologer?

Rajesh: What about blind faith?

Sri Sri: Faith is faith…it cannot be blind. What you call blind is not faith—at least not yours!

Blindness and faith cannot meet. It is when you lose faith that you become blind.

News Flash

The swamis from Adichunchunagiri Math arrived at our German Academy with a grand Satsang on Friday night and a picnic to the nearby waterfall on Sunday.

Mumbai: Four thousand people filled a beautiful hall for a fabulous Satsang and meditation led by Sri Sri. The sound system had the hiccups(!), but miraculously delivered crystal clear sound whenever Sri Sri spoke.

This Weekly Knowledge was written on the way to a spontaneous Satsang of 600 people, after which Sri Sri returned to Bangalore.

September 10, 1997
Bangalore Ashram, India

118 How to Get Centered

Shift your awareness from the experience to the experiencer. All experiences are on the circumference; they keep on changing. The unchanging experiencer is at the center. Again and again, come back to the experiencer.

If you are frustrated, instead of spending all your time on the experience of frustration, ask, "Who is frustrated?"

If you are unhappy, ask, "Who is unhappy?"

If you think you know something, ask, "Who knows?" *(laughter)*

If you think you are enlightened, ask, "Who is it that is enlightened?"

If you think you are ignorant, ask, "Who is ignorant?"

If you think *poor me*, ask, "Who is 'poor me?'"

If you think you are highly devoted, ask, "Who is it that is devoted?"

Shed all your faces and face the I. Then you have truly come to me!

✍ News Flash

In Pune, the Chief Minister of Maharashtra conferred the Guru Mahatmya Award upon Sri Sri for outstanding contribution to humanity.

September 17, 1997
Bangalore Ashram, India

119 The Five Insights

*L*OVE IS YOUR NATURE.

When love finds an expression, you often get caught up in the object. Your sight is caught outside. To return back to your nature, you need insight.

Pain is the first insight. It takes you away from the object and turns you towards your body and mind.

Energy is the second insight. A bolt of energy brings you back to your Self.

Divine love is the third insight. A glimpse makes you so complete and overrules all relative pleasures.

Ecstasy is the fourth insight. An elevation of consciousness with partial awareness of physical reality is ecstasy.

Non-dual awareness is the fifth insight, the realization that all is made up of One and only One.

When love glows, it is bliss.
When love flows, it is compassion.
When love blows, it is anger.
When love ferments, it is jealousy.
When love is all "no's," it is hatred.
When love acts, it is perfection.
When love knows, it is ME!

✏️ News Flash

Satsang groups are launching service projects, including free medical aid, sanitation, and housing for the poor, and blood donation camps. Every Satsang group is asked to take up seva projects, keeping aside personal likes and dislikes.

September 24, 1997
Bangalore Ashram, India

120 Five Signs of the Satguru*

*I*N THE PRESENCE OF THE SATGURU:

1. Knowledge flourishes
2. Sorrow diminishes
3. Joy wells up without any reason
4. Lack diminishes; abundance dawns
5. All talents manifest

To the degree you feel connected to the Master, these qualities manifest in your life.

Sit with your eyes closed and feel your connection with the Master.

*Master of Truth, the One who leads you all the way to Enlightenment

✎ News Flash

Renowned saints from all over India are visiting the Ashram. A series of Advanced Courses ended in tears of joy, followed by a brief respite for the Ashram volunteers.

Guruji was a guest of honor with 15,000 people at the Adichunchunagiri ashram.

Preparations have begun for Navaratri (Nine Nights of Mother Divine).

Exercises for this week:
   1. Make a knowledge sheet.
   2. Make a commitment for a seva project. The more you give, the more strength will be given to you.
   3. Sit with your eyes closed for one minute and surrender your name. How do you feel...? Dissolving the name is awareness; dissolving the form is meditation. The world is name and form; bliss transcends name and form.

October 1, 1997
Bangalore Ashram, India

121 Six Signs of a Seeker

1. An acknowledgement that one knows very little
Many people think they know—without knowing. They get stuck in their limited knowledge. They never learn. The first thing a seeker knows is that he knows very little.

2. A willingness to learn
Many people acknowledge that they do not know, but they are not ready to learn.

3. Non-judgmental and open-minded
Some people would like to learn, but their close-minded and judgmental attitudes do not allow them.

4. A total, one-pointed commitment to the Path
Some people are open-minded, but they lack commitment and one-pointedness. They keep shopping here and there and never progress on one path.

5. Always puts truth and service before pleasure
Sometimes even committed and one-pointed people stray from the path in pursuit of momentary pleasures.

6. Patience and perseverance
Some people are committed, one-pointed, and are not swayed by pleasures, but if they lack patience and perseverance, they become restless and dejected.

✎ **News Flash**

The festival of Navaratri has begun. Yagyas are being conducted during these nine days for the peace, prosperity, health, and happiness of all devotees (present and future!). More about yagyas next week.

Swami Pragyanandji, the renowned saint, is at the Ashram giving discourses on the Shrimad Bhagavatam, *as Guruji is in silence.*

October 8, 1997
Bangalore Ashram, India

122 Yagyas

*Y*AGYAS ARE THE ANCIENT METHOD OF ENRICHING the subtle and to purify individual and collective consciousness.

Yagyas have three aspects:

1. **Deva Puja:** Honoring the Divine in all forms

2. **Sangatikarana:** Hastening the process of evolution by unifying all the elements and people in creation

3. **Dana:** Sharing with others; giving freely what one has been blessed with

✐ News Flash

The depth of Sri Sri's silence contrasted sharply with the noisy, boisterous celebration. Activities started early in the morning and finished late at night. The meditation hall became a feast for the senses with Vedic chanting, the beat of drums, loud clarinets, the visiting swamis, and the usual ecstatic bhajans. The Ashram was fully lit and so were the faces. The poor from seven villages received new clothes and gifts; for many it was their first gift of new garments in their life and there was such gratitude. While the rich fasted and prayed, the poor feasted in this genuine celebration.

October 16, 1997
Bangalore Ashram, India

123 God as a Child

You have always thought of God as a father, up in the heavens somewhere. But can you see God as a child?

When you think of God as a father, you will want to demand and take from Him. But when you see God as a child, you have no demands.

God is the very core of your existence. You are pregnant with God. You have to take care of your pregnancy and deliver this Child into the world. Most people do not deliver. Whosoever delivers can also grant wishes.

God is your child who clings onto you like a baby 'til you grow old and die. This Child clings onto the devotee, crying for nourishment. Sadhana, satsang, and seva are the nourishment.

Belma: You cannot pray to a child; you can only pray to your father.

Sri Sri: Why do you want to pray? What do you want to ask? A good father already knows what to give.

Belma: But what about surrender?

Sri Sri: Your surrender to a child is more authentic because there is no demand.

Take care of your God! Atheists lurk around the corner! Doubts, disbelief, and ignorance are the atheists in your mind—so better take care!

News Flash

Like a bolt of lightning, the climax of the Navaratri celebrations came at high voltage. Even the learned pundits were visibly moved. At the grand finale, the Ashram reverberated with enormous energy, leaving everyone spellbound.

Devotees accompanied Sri Sri on a visit to a village an hour away where we are providing shelter and self-employment training to the neediest of the women.

An Advanced Course has begun at the Ashram. This weekend Sri Sri will tour the south, where a Satsang will be held in his honor in Shimoga—the town where Guruji conducted his first course fifteen years ago.

October 23, 1997
Highway 7, between Bangalore and Shimoga, India

124 Feel Blessed

BREAK THROUGH ALL THE BARRIERS AND FEEL you are blessed. This is the one and only step you have to take—the rest will all happen.

This deep sense of feeling *I am blessed* can help you overcome all obstacles in life. You receive courage and confidence and you will open up for grace to pour in.

Once you realize you are blessed, then:
▲ All complaints disappear
▲ All grumblings disappear
▲ All insecurities disappear
▲ A sense of feeling unloved disappears
▲ Wanting love disappears

If you don't realize you are blessed, then doership begins.

To make a difference in your life, feel you are blessed. Especially for those on this path of Knowledge, there is every reason for you to feel blessed.

Feel you are blessed.
This is the first step towards the Self.

✎ News Flash

Thousands thronged two Satsangs in Coimbatore to glimpse Sri Sri. What a treat to experience 1800 people doing pranayama and Kriya together!

On the way to Shimoga, Sri Sri visited the Temple of Mother Divine and was received with full honor. The Master arrived at Shimoga for a touching reunion with longtime devotees and a grand Satsang. Saints from various ashrams greeted Sri Sri and all the devotees with warmth and enthusiasm. The entire village came out dancing to receive the Master with a 20-foot electric chariot strung with thousands of lights. (Guruji looked embarrassed!)

October 30, 1997
Rishikesh, India

125 Diwali

*T*IME AND SPACE ARE INFINITE. GRAINS OF SAND ARE countless. Atoms in the universe are innumerable. So also are the stars, the galaxies.

The same is with life on this planet. There is neither a beginning nor an end, because all is spherical. A sphere has no beginning and no end, no goal or direction.

Truth has no direction, no goal. Truth itself is the goal, and Truth is infinite.

Feeling and experiencing infinity within this finite body, living timelessness within the timespan of life, uncovering bliss within the misery—this is what you are here for.

When this wisdom dawns, it gives rise to celebration. However, in celebration you may lose your focus or awareness. The ancient rishis knew this, so to maintain awareness amidst the gaiety of celebration, they brought sacredness and puja to every event.

Today is Diwali, the Festival of Lights. The streets and buildings are lit up with colorful lights.

The four aspects of Diwali are:
1. Lights—symbolizing the spreading of Knowledge
2. Firecrackers—Watching the firecrackers gives a relief to the explosive tendencies inside. When the explosion happens outside, the explosion inside is diffused.
3. Gifts and sweets—Sharing gifts and distributing

sweets dispels bitterness and renews friendships.

4. Abundance—Feeling a sense of abundance brings awareness and gratefulness for what one has.

Celebrate the Knowledge and feel the abundance. Those who have will be given more!

✎ News Flash

The Ashram hosted a Family Day for local course graduates while guests were introduced to the Knowledge. A Maha-Kriya for 2000 and lunch for 4000 had volunteers jumping and dancing by the end of the day.

After Satsang in Pune, crowds crushed onto the stage for darshan with Sri Sri as volunteers barely managed the enthusiastic mob. Thousands of pairs of neatly packaged and numbered shoes left at the entryway were trampled by the stampede that followed. Many people lost their shoes but were too happy to care.

Next morning, despite a peak-season Diwali business day, 1,800 course graduates joined Guruji for Satsang.

Sixty blind women began a week-long residence course at the Bangalore Ashram.

November 6, 1997
Rishikesh, India

126 Love is Your Very Existence

*S*UPPOSE SOMEONE SHOWS YOU A LOT OF LOVE. WHAT do you do?

1. You do not know how to respond.
2. You feel obliged and bound.
3. You shrink or shy away.
4. You feel foolish and awkward.
5. You try to reciprocate even though it is not genuine.
6. You doubt the love expressed or your worthiness.
7. You become afraid of losing respect, because respect maintains a distance and love does not allow distance.
8. Your ego hardens and does not allow you to receive and reciprocate.
9. Anything else_____*(fill in the blank)*

The ability to receive love comes with the ability to give love. The more you are centered and, by experience, know that you are love, the more you will feel at home with any amount of love that is expressed in any manner. Deep inside, you will know:

Love is not an emotion!
Love is your very existence!

✎ News Flash

Diwali celebrations continue with candlelight Satsangs in the Valley of the Saints. Advanced Course participants broke all boundaries of course structure as 200 people dropped in unannounced! Thanks to the volunteers, smiles prevailed on all 500 faces. Course participants also cleaned up tons of garbage from the banks of the Ganges.

Indian teachers and organizers have resolved to start the following Sri Sri Seva Projects, and all Satsang groups are invited to join:

1. Donate a minimum of 2% of personal income towards rural development and hygiene;

2. Contact supermarkets/stores and encourage them to use paper or cloth bags instead of plastic.

November 13, 1997
Jaipur, India

127 Your Expressions of Love

YOU FEEL A LOT OF LOVE FOR SOMEONE AND THEY do not take it. What do you do?

▼ Get frustrated
▼ Turn the love into hatred and wish for revenge
▼ Again and again remind them how much you love them and how little they love you
▼ Become fussy and cranky
▼ Throw tantrums
▼ Feel humiliated and try to protect your respect
▼ Resolve never to love again
▼ Feel hurt and mistreated
▼ Try to be aloof and indifferent

...and you have seen that none of these work! They only make it worse.

What is the way out of this? How can you maintain your lovingness?

▲ Have patience.
▲ Be centered and limit your expression of love. Sometimes over-expression of love puts people off.
▲ Change your expression of love.
▲ Take it for granted that they love you and accept their style of expression. Like a mother with three kids—one child talks, one child does not talk, one child throws

tantrums—her love for each child is constant regardless of their behavior.
- ▲ Genuinely acknowledge their love for you. This will turn your demand into gratefulness, and the more you are grateful in life, the more love comes your way.
- ▲ Know that hurt is part of love and take responsibility for it.
- ▲ Realize that when you move away from your center, you will feel miserable and that the nature of worldliness is misery.

News Flash

On the Rishikesh course, deafening joy chased the silence into the mountains.

In New Delhi, a packed audience welcomed Sri Sri to Siri Fort, the country's most prestigious auditorium.

Devotees in the Pink City of Jaipur crowned Sri Sri with a turban and celebrated his visit in warm, friendly, and colorful Rajasthani style.

November 20, 1997
Bangalore Ashram, India

128 Ego

When is there ego?

1. When you don't get attention.
2. When you seem to be losing attention.
3. When you get attention. *(laughter)*

Ego causes heaviness, discomfort, fear, anxiety. Ego doesn't let love flow.

Ego is separateness, non-belongingness, wanting to prove and to possess.

Ego can be transcended by knowing the Truth, by inquiring "Who am I?"

Often you feel contempt or jealousy towards someone with ego. Instead you should have compassion.

Ego has a positive aspect: ego drives one to do work. A person can do a job out of joy, compassion, or out of ego. Most of the work in the society is for boosting the ego. In Satsang, work is done out of love.

When you wake up and see that there is nothing to be proved and nothing to possess, ego dissolves.

✎ News Flash

The Satsang tour continued on to Hyderabad, where despite a cyclone warning, swarms of people came to be blessed by the Master and were surprised to hear him speaking chaste Telugu. Many healing experiences were shared. Sri Sri's talk to doctors on the next day was simply stunning and, as with all his best talks, it was not recorded!

Fireworks and exuberant devotees welcomed Guruji back to Bangalore. An Advanced Course is in progress and preparations are on for a big public Satsang in Bangalore on the twenty third.

November 27, 1997
Bangalore Ashram, India

129 Memory

*M*EMORY MAKES YOU MISERABLE OR WISE.

Memory of experiences and events in the ever-changing world—however good or bad—constrict the vastness of the Self. They bind you.

Memory of your nature—the non-changing Self—expands and elevates awareness. This liberates you.

You are what you are because of your memory. If you are ignorant, it is because of your memory. If you are enlightened, it is because of your memory.

Forgetfulness of the Infinite is misery. Forgetfulness of the trivial is ecstasy.

Question: How do we get rid of unpleasant memories and limitations?

Sri Sri:
- ▲ Know the impermanent nature of the world and events.
- ▲ Realize that past events do not exist in the present.
- ▲ Accept the past and drop it.
- ▲ Be dispassionate and centered.
- ▲ Memory of the Self is gained in the company and service of the Enlightened.
- ▲ *So Ham!* Increase prana.
- ▲ *So what?!!*
- ▲ If none of this works—*then go to the moon!!!*

News Flash

Sri Sri was the chief guest of a congregation of the Lions Clubs of Karnataka, attended by many dignitaries, where a number of service projects were initiated.

A massive rally was organized for environmental awareness in Bangalore, followed by a huge Satsang where Sri Sri had everyone mesmerized as usual.

Guruji escaped for a short trip to Delhi, leaving people at the Ashram surprised.

Baba Avtar Hari Maharaj, a renowned saint from Hardwar, is visiting the Ashram.

December 3, 1997
Calicut, India

130 Intellect

THE INTELLECT HARBORS INHIBITIONS, LIKES AND dislikes, approvals and disapprovals. The intellect also harbors wisdom, which brings forth intuition.

Question: Is intuition beyond intellect?
Sri Sri: Yes, but it shines through the intellect.
Question: Are emotions and intellect contradictory?
Sri Sri: They can be contradictory.
Question: When there is a conflict, which is better?
Sri Sri: In conflict, there is no better conflict!

The pure intellect is not caught up in the emotional turbulence of the mind. The pure intellect rises beyond conflicts.

Usually the intellect gets colored by emotions and becomes impure, like muddy water. Then it is unable to reflect the Self. A pure intellect, still and serene, reflects the Self.

Question: Is intellect affected by karma?
Sri Sri: Karma does not afflict the pure intellect. Liberation purifies the intellect. The sanskrit word for intellect is *buddhi*; one who is liberated is a buddha.

✎ News Flash

Sri Avtar Hari blessed the Ashram and stayed with Guruji for three days.

People from Russia, Poland, China, and other countries went on a trip to Kerala with Guruji. Six thousand people gathered at the first stop at Thiruvananthapuram, the state capital.

At Cochin, the open ground by the seaside was fabulously decorated. Caparisoned elephants in traditional style, angels, flowers, and lamps accorded a warm welcome. The grounds packed in ten thousand people—imagine how much time it took for the darshan line!

In Thrissur, the cultural capital of Kerala, five thousand gathered for a grand Satsang at an indoor stadium. The teamwork at Thrissur was a unique example for all; this time around, the volunteers felt no pressure—they did less and accomplished more.

With not space even for an ant to crawl at the biggest auditorium in Calicut, many had to be content watching the Satsang on the closed circuit television outside.

Many healing experiences were reported during the Satsangs.

Guruji is back at the Bangalore Ashram for another fortnight.

December 10, 1997
Bangalore Ashram, India

131 Time and Mind

When you are happy, the mind expands; then time appears too short.

When you are unhappy, the mind contracts; then time appears too long.

When the mind has equanimity, you transcend time.

To escape from time, many resort to alcohol, sleep, etc., but when the mind is dull or unconscious, it is unable to experience the Self.

Samadhi (no-mindedness, timelessness) is the real peace. A few moments of samadhi gives the mind a lot of energy. This is the greatest healer.

A thought is nothing but a ripple in this moment of time. This moment also has a mind of its own—a Big Mind which has infinite organizing power.

Before you fall into slumber and as soon as you wake up from sleep, in the moments of twilight of consciousness, experience this timelessness beyond mind!

🔊 News Flash

In Apple Valley, California, 80 homeless children received gifts at a special Christmas party.

In the slums in Mumbai, India, Satsangs and seva projects have begun.

A blood donation camp was organized in Surat.

Some people in the surrounding villages of the Ashram were given free housing.

At Satsang, someone suggested that we have some deer, peacocks, swans, and doves at the Ashram. Sri Sri promptly answered, "You are all dear to me! You are peacocks because you dance! Like swans you have vivek—the power of discrimination—and like doves you carry the message of peace to the world!"

December 18, 1997
Bangalore Ashram, India

132 Faces of Infinity

*Y*OU HAVE MANY FACES, ONLY YOU DON'T FACE them. When you come face to face with your faces, then conflicts, confusion, and chaos arise in you.

From time to time, in different phases, different faces appear. As you come close to your Being, all faces melt and leave you as the Space that you are.

At the gross level, you identify yourself as somebody.

As you move to more subtle levels, you may identify yourself as some energy, or an incarnation of some angel, saint, or prophet.

When you go beyond even this identity, you are whole, holy, the Brahman—Purna Brahman Narayana.

✍ News Flash

The Ashram bid farewell to the Russians, but Southeast Asians, Southern Africans, Malaysians, and a LOT of Indians from all directions occupy every available space.

Amidst the hectic activity at the Ashram, there is deep silence and serenity. The Advanced Course, TTC, Sahaj Samadhi, Basic Course, and ART Excel are all in full swing.

December 24, 1997
German Academy

133 Celebration and the Christmas Tree

HUMAN LIFE IS A COMBINATION OF BODY (MATTER) and spirit (vibration). Isn't it?

Joy is forgetting that you are matter and becoming an intense vibration.

Carnal instincts also make you feel intense vibrations momentarily, and that's how they give a glimpse of joy. But the thing is, this joy is short-lived and it makes you dense later on.

Pleasure that comes from Satsang is of a higher nature. Mantras and singing create vibrations in the spirit. That's why when you sing, the ecstasy stays for a long time.

Pleasure from the gross is short-lived, tiring and binding. Pleasure in the subtle is long lasting, energizing, refreshing, and freeing.

When you know you are electricity (vibration/energy), then craving, greed, lust, and anger disappear. Then you become a true celebration.

Message for Christmas:
You are the Christmas tree that points upwards with branches on all sides. At the time of year when other trees are barren, you are green with many gifts to offer.

You bear gifts and lights—not for yourself, but for others. Remember that all the gifts you are carrying in your life are for others. Anyone who comes to you, offer them your gifts.

There were lots of presents around Sri Sri's couch. John asked, "Are you going to open the gifts?" Sri Sri winked, pointed at the people and replied, "I am always opening the gifts."

Your life is a gift. And you have come to unwrap this gift. In the process of unwrapping, remember to also save the wrapping papers. Your whole environment, situations, circumstances, and body are the wrapping papers.

Often when we unwrap, we tear the wrapping papers. At times we are in such a hurry that we even destroy the gifts. With patience and endurance, open your gifts—and save the wrappers!

✎ News Flash

As hectic activities continued in the Bangalore Ashram, Sri Sri moved on to Madras for a huge Satsang. Then he went to Delhi where he met with the Vice President of India. An unscheduled Satsang of 1,200 devotees gathered just by word of mouth! That same night Sri Sri left for Germany.

Every corridor and corner of the German Academy wears a festive look. Smiles from people of 18 countries are the moving decorations. The seva team transformed the Academy into a warm and cozy home.

Many of the nicely wrapped gift boxes of various sizes given to Sri Sri were found to be hollow and empty!

New Year's Eve, 1997
German Academy

134 A Wise Person is Happy Even in Bad Times

People who serve will have good times even in bad times.

When there is famine or war, Red Cross people will be fine because they are serving. The more relief they can bring to others, the happier they feel.

On the other hand, selfish people who just want to enjoy for themselves will be miserable even in good times.

In good times, people often lose their happiness over some small thing. Hosts often do not enjoy their parties because some little thing is missing, they forgot to invite somebody, somebody did not come, or some little thing went wrong.

A wise person is happy even in bad times. A stupid person is unhappy even in good times.

YOU make the time good or bad. People usually blame the bad time and then wait for a good time. But even if an astrologer says you are in a hopeless time, you can make it good!

Like weather, time has its own impact on you. Your satsangs and sadhana are your shield, your protection!

Realize that you are more than time and that you can move through time with your timeless connection to the Divine.

Don't feel shy to speak about human and spiritual values. The time has come now to call the whole world!

The ALL is calling,
The ball is rolling!
Time is milling,
The soul is willing...

A new New Year's greeting: BE EVER NEW, HAPPY YOU!

✍ News Flash

The first Advanced Course has finished in Germany and the second one has begun. Reports of service activities have come from various parts of the world.

January 7, 1998
Milano, Italy

135 You are Pure Electricity

*D*ESIRES FOR SENSORY PLEASURE ARE ELECTRIC in nature; they get neutralized as they move toward the objects of the senses.

If by your skill you could move desires within you—toward the center of your existence—another dimension of everlasting pleasure, thrill, bliss, and undying love will all be yours.

Lust, greed, and jealousy are powerful because they are nothing but energy—and *you* are the source of it, pure electricity. Dedication and devotion keep your electricity pure and move you upward. When you realize you *yourself* are the electricity of pleasure, your cravings subside and serenity dawns. Also, remembering that you will die makes you alive now, free from cravings and aversions.

The wise ones are always careful not to get their minds entangled and dizzy.

✏ News Flash

People from 22 countries took part in the Advanced Course in Germany thanks to the simultaneous translation system. Sri Sri spoke on spiritual dimensions the entire week.

After a fantastic talk at a packed Milano auditorium, everyone held a baccara rose in their hand as they went out with a smile.

Sri Sri is off to Slovenia and Croatia for a two-day visit. Amma* turns 70 this week; her birthday will be celebrated in Bangalore on the twelfth with a distribution of blankets and food to the poor.

*Sri Sri's mother

January 14, 1998
Paramaribo, Surinam

136 Politics

Don't let politics sway you away from the Path. If you are afraid of politics, you cannot be successful in the spiritual realm.

You have to cross the barricade of politics. It is the test of your strength, your commitment, and your focus. You cannot avoid politics, but whether or not to harbor politics in your mind is your choice.

There were politics among the twelve apostles and also around Buddha. Krishna was in politics from head to toe. And you say *you* don't want politics? The greater your aversion, the more you harbor in your consciousness.

When you recognize politics in any group or satsang, that is a blessing, an opportunity for you to be centered and go inward. You will not blame the group, run away from people, or chicken out, and you will enhance your skill to act while being unattached.

Advantages of politics:
▲ Brings up diversity in people
▲ Lets you see different viewpoints, ways, and tendencies
▲ Enhances your skill to communicate and act
▲ Brings centeredness and dispassion
▲ Shakes you up and makes you apply the Knowledge
▲ Enhances your capacity to accept and tolerate
▲ Makes you realize that this whole life is a game

The strong will smile through politics while the weak will lament.

Cross the threshold of politics and come to the Divine.

✍ News Flash

Sri Sri arrived in time to address the inter-religious conference organized by the parliamentarians of Croatia, followed by Satsang at the beautiful Sheraton Hotel, filled to capacity. Sri Sri met with many dignitaries, and TV people from Croatia filmed a documentary.

In Trinidad, the Prime Minister and two other cabinet ministers met with Sri Sri, expressing their gratitude for our work, and offering their wholehearted support. One of the ministers recalled Guruji's comment last year that the Prime Minister would become spiritual, which he did.

Now the telephones in serene Surinam are ringing off the hook! More than 300 people have already registered for the Basic Course and they haven't even met Sri Sri yet. The receptionist, the watchman, even the housekeepers are all busy doing one job: enrolling the people!

January 21, 1998
Williams Island, Florida

137 Tolerance and Acceptance are Not Virtues

*M*ANY PEOPLE THINK TOLERANCE IS A VIRTUE.
Tolerance is a negative term. Tolerance indicates a deep sense of dislike. If you like something, there is no question about whether you tolerate it.

When you are tolerating something, it means you are temporarily putting up with it. Tolerance is a potential volcano. If you are tolerating, it means you are still holding on to something.

At any time tolerance can turn into hatred. Tolerance indicates a sense of separateness, small mindedness, limited awareness.

Acceptance is also negative. You accept only that which is not lovable.

Question: Do you need self-assurance to love people?
Sri Sri: Only the Self is always assuring—nothing else! This is our company—the Self-Assurance Company.

Question: Aren't we supposed to accept people as they are?
Sri Sri: If you don't love them, then you will have to accept them.

These words *tolerance* and *acceptance* are thought to be positive; I say they are not. Tolerance and acceptance come with judgment and separation.

Don't accept people as they are or tolerate them. Just love them as they are.

🖊 News Flash

From Surinam, the entourage moved on to Bogota, the capital of Columbia. After an interview for national television, the host of the show said she has to change her whole series, which was entitled "Tolerance."

Bewildered organizers were unprepared for the huge crowds at the evening talk.

In Panama, a minute-by-minute program was put together by Martine and her team. The celebration moved on to Costa Rica for a day, where, in contrast, the hall had enough space for three seats per person. Satsangs were just a dozen devotees, and Sri Sri fed them all.

In Florida, Guruji commented from the beautiful 28th floor accommodations, "I am staying in the second best place, the first being my Self!" Ronnie Newman organized a fabulous event sponsored by the Crime Prevention Unit of Nova Southeastern University, attended by scientists, researchers, therapists, and justice personnel.

January 28, 1998
Santa Monica, California

138 False Security

*F*ALSE SECURITY DOES NOT ALLOW YOUR FAITH TO grow. Faith grows only when you have dropped your securities.

False security is keeping faith where it doesn't belong. It is the illusion of security in having a job, a house, friends.

Even if you have all the material securities, without faith you will still reel in fear. When you buffer your life with securities, you keep faith away.

Faith is your greatest security. Faith brings perfection in you.

Keep money in the bank or in the pocket, not in the mind. Keep the house where it belongs, not in the mind. Keep friends and family where they belong, not in the mind. You have to let go of all possessions in the mind.

Your body belongs to the world.
Your spirit belongs to the Divine.
The Divine is your only security.

Faith is realizing that you always get what you need. Faith is giving the Divine a chance to act.

✎ News Flash

In the car to Verna's house after Satsang, Kumi said, "Lets take the long way home!" Guruji replied, "I am making the ride home short, yet you want to take a long ride!"

Sri Sri gave a brilliant talk to over 200 people at the "World's Great Religions and Their Transformation in the 21st Century" symposium at the University of California, Los Angeles.

The Santa Monica Satsangs were filled with laughter, brilliant questions, and even more brilliant answers. Divya's voice lifted everyone's hearts.

One evening Scott invited over 80 people to come for the first time to hear Sri Sri speak, but Guruji did not say a word. Instead, he gave the entire talk in his own version of sign language. It was hilarious. Deaf people who were present shed tears at Sri Sri's intuitive understanding of sign language.

David said, "Guruji, you travel and work so much—20 countries in one month! Do you ever take a vacation?" Sri Sri said, "In between lifetimes!"

February 3, 1998
Kaua'i, Hawaii

139 Organization and Devotion

*O*RGANIZATION IS CONTROL. DEVOTION IS CHAOS! Organization needs attention to details, a material awareness; organization is being worldly. Devotion is getting lost, forgetting the world, being in ecstasy.

These are opposite in nature. They don't go together, yet they cannot be apart or exist without the other.

No organization can arise without devotion. When you have so much devotion, you want to organize. Devotion brings faith, compassion, responsibility, and a desire to share knowledge, wisdom, and love. Then organization happens. Organization exists through devotion.

If you are devoted, you won't just sit. The nature of devotion is to give. If you think you are devoted and you are not caring for the world, then you are merely selfish. Real devotion means being one with the Divine, and the Divine cares for the world.

Often you lose devotion in organizing. And in the name of devotion you create chaos or disregard the organization.

You have to be a saint to be in devotion AND in an organization. With both, you are on the mark.

So...get lost—and be guided!

News Flash

Sri Sri received a royal Hawaiian welcome from many new devotees when he arrived on the island of Oahu. John Osborne spoke on a local TV health show, and the largest course ever on Oahu was taught in Sri Sri's presence.

Satsangs continue on the Garden Island of Kauai, where Guruji was ready for an adventure in the huge waves—but found himself surrounded by devotees at a safe beach instead.

February 12, 1998
Singapore

140 When a Mistake is Not a Mistake

BLESSED ARE THOSE WHO DON'T SEE A MISTAKE AS a mistake...!!!

When you make a *new* mistake, it is not a mistake—you have learned a valuable lesson. But when you keep doing the same mistake over and over, it is a BIG mistake.

A mistake is something that brings misery to you in the long run, so why would someone knowingly commit a mistake? A "mistake" simply means you have "missed taking" a lesson that has come your way. Do not lament over your mistake. Just take the lesson from it.

It is hard not to see your own mistake. Outwardly you may justify yourself or plead innocence to someone else, but a mistake pricks your conscience.

Do not justify yourself. Instead, feel the prick of the mistake. That prick takes you out of the mistake.

When you point out a mistake to someone, do you see him as separate from you, or do you make him feel a part of you? Do your words make him more stressed, or do they create more awareness in that person?

Often you do not point out a mistake when it is required. This is also a mistake. Pointing out a mistake without consideration to time and place is also a mistake.

The fool keeps making the same mistakes again and again and never learns from them. Wise is the one who learns from his own mistakes. Wisest is the one who learns from others' mistakes!

You will not be judged by your mistakes, but by your virtues.
   Mistakes are of the earth.
   Virtues are of the Divine.

✎ News Flash

In Bali, we visited the ancient temple of Besaki, where, as in the old days, there is only the empty seat of the deity, signifying the Divine beyond form.

The Indonesian Director of Religious Affairs and a member of the Ministry of Education welcomed Sri Sri at the opening of our Jakarta Ashram.

Devotees from Jakarta have adopted an orphanage in Puncak. The director of the orphanage said that while other people bring money, clothes, and toys, our group supplied the missing nutrient the children need the most: love! The children also received packages of school supplies and goodies. We all laughed, sang, and danced as the director cried tears of gratitude.

The entourage moved to Singapore where more than 1000 people welcomed Sri Sri at the packed SLF Auditorium. The evening commenced with a traditional Chinese lion dance. Later, Sri Sri gave practical points on "Awakening the Beauty Within You."

February 18, 1998
Bangalore, India

141 **Respect**

When someone respects you, it is not because *you* possess some virtues; it is because of *their* greatness.

If you say God is great, it means YOU are great. God is already great—your saying so doesn't affect God.

When you respect someone, it shows your own magnanimity. However many people you don't respect in the world, that much less is your wealth. If you respect everyone, that much more is your value. Wise is the one who respects everyone.

Question: But Gurudev, you can't respect a terrorist!

Sri Sri: You have to respect a terrorist, too, because he shows you the right way at his own cost.

Respect is a quality of refined consciousness. Respect for the Self is faith; faith is being open.

If you are open, you are close to me!
If you are close to me, you cannot but open up!

✎ News Flash

Bhanu greeted the entourage with smiles and roses as we arrived in India at 1:30 AM. Touring through all the Ashram facilities, Guruji personally saw to each one's comfort and accommodations until well past dawn.

The second symposium of the International Association for Human Values inspired people from 30 countries. Messages arrived from world leaders expressing their support and gratitude. A lecture on Ayurveda and talks by eminent spiritual leaders rounded out the program.

February 24, 1998
Bangalore, India

142 Shiva and Vashi

OFTEN PEOPLE THINK THEY ARE IN CONTROL OF their life, their situation, their world.

Control is an illusion.

The whole world moves according to the laws of Nature in an auspicious rhythm of innocence, intelligence, and divinity. That is Shiva.

Shiva is the eternal state of Being, the One without a second, the harmonious innocence that knows no control.

Control is Vashi—Shiva reversed. Vashi is of the mind. Vashi is weakness. Vashi is doing something by exerting unnatural pressure.

Vashi requires two, and duality is the cause of fear. Shiva, that harmonious innocence, dissolves duality.

Shiva means wholeness of the moment.
When there is no regret of past, no want of future, the moment is whole and complete.
Time stops, mind stops.

✎ News Flash

The International Association for Human Values conference continues.

The Ayurvedic Clinic is dispensing knowledge and remedies day and night.

In Sri Sri's presence, live music performances under Sumeru's starry canopy enchanted us with recitals for sitar, bamboo flute, and Indian classical dance.

A number of devotees took a side trip to Mysore to visit the palace, Brindavan Gardens, the Mother Divine temple, and a school for the blind.

Last night's dinner featured a smorgasbord of Indian cuisine from around the country.

Today is Shivaratri. Devotees are flocking to the Ashram to witness the yagyas and receive the Master's darshan.

March 4, 1998
Rishikesh, India

143 Formality and Cordiality

YOU CANNOT ELIMINATE FORMALITY IN SOCIETY.
It has its place. Formality improves communication. Yet communication is only necessary when there are two. Formality maintains duality.

Cordiality improves communion—oneness. Without cordiality, formality can be hypocritical and may appear uncaring.

Organizational structures are based on formality. An organization cannot begin and orderliness cannot prevail if formalities are abandoned. All your plans of action are measured steps of formality.

Cordiality is one's nature, the core of one's existence; formality is the outer shell. When the outer shell is thin, like the shade of a lamp, the inner light can shine forth. But if the shade is too opaque, you cannot see the light.

Love and knowledge are rooted in cordiality. For these to blossom, you need an informal, cordial environment.

Devotion is informal...and totally chaotic.
So, strike a balance between cordial formality and formal cordiality!

✎ News Flash

Two planeloads of devotees flew en-masse to Ahmedabad where their hosts greeted them with singing and dancing at the airport, followed by dinner in a traditional Indian village setting and a riotous Satsang. The next morning, devotees joined in a Maha Kriya of more than 3000, personally led by Sri Sri. Many toured Mahatma Gandhi's ashram, and the unforgettable day ended with a Maha Satsang of over 20,000. Darshan alone took four hours!

The group traveled north to new course facilities at an ashram in Rishikesh. At sunset, Sri Sri led a dip in the Ganges. Devotees launched floating ghee lamps from the river banks to honor the auspicious occasion. The program continues in silence with visiting saints, profoundly deep meditations, and new levels of knowledge and experience.

March 11, 1998
Rishikesh, India

144 You are the Tenth

Ten people were walking on foot from one village to another. On the way, they had to cross a river. Reaching the other shore, they wanted to be sure all had crossed safely. Each one counted only nine and left himself out. They were very distraught and began to cry for the loss of the tenth.

A wise man came along and asked them "Oh, my dear friends, why are you crying?"

"We were ten but now we are only nine," they replied.

The wise man saw that they were ten, so he made them stand and count. To the last person he said, "You are the tenth!" They all rejoiced for having regained the tenth.

The five senses and the four inner faculties (mind, intellect, memory, ego) all lament when they lose sight of the Self. Then the Master comes and shows you that YOU are the tenth!

Count, but never stop until you find the tenth.

Finding the ever-present Self inside makes everything truly joyful.

Question: What did Brahma think when he made this creation?

Sri Sri: He didn't think before doing, He didn't take anyone's suggestion. I would have given Him a few!

📣 News Flash

Bhajans coming out from a locked suitcase! Was it a miracle? No...a tape recorder inside got turned on, delighting the late-night volunteers.

The course ended with the whole group joining Sri Sri for another dip in the Ganges. An Advanced Course with 400 participants is now under way in Rishikesh while TTC 1 and 2 are having a hilarious time. Everyone is gearing up for Holi, the Festival of Colors.

March 19, 1998
Rishikesh, India

145 Inside Out

OFTEN PEOPLE SAY, "BE THE SAME OUTSIDE AS WHAT you are inside." I ask you, how is this possible?

Inside you are a vast ocean, an infinite sky. Outside you are finite—just a small limited form, a normal stupid person!

All that you are inside—the love, the beauty, the compassion, the Divinity—doesn't show up fully outside. What shows is only the crust of behaviors.

Ask yourself, "Am I really my behavioral patterns?" "Am I really this limited body/mind complex?" No...you are not the same inside as outside.

Don't mistake the outer crust for who you are inside.
And don't show your infinite lordship outside, for Divinity is not easily understood.
Let there be some mystery.

✎ News Flash

Saints, merchants, and prominent people of Rishikesh joined our course participants to celebrate Holi, the Festival of Colors. With saints clad in orange and Sri Sri in white, Guruji said, "The heart is white, the sign of purity in life; the head is orange, the symbol of sacrifice; and life is all colorful!"

Later in the week Sri Sri met with the Shankaracharya and other saints.

The Bangalore Ashram school celebrated its Annual School Day with parents and local dignitaries in attendance.

Among the healings reported this week from those practicing Sudarshan Kriya:

▲ *A 56-year old man who had lost his vision reported he can now read the newspaper.*

▲ *A man who suffered from abnormal blood pressure for 10-12 years was found to have normal blood pressure.*

▲ *The mother-in-law of a devotee, a 65-year old woman who has not even taken the course, had a brain hemorrhage and multiple injuries caused by a fall. She was hospitalized on January 10 and by March 2 showed no improvement. Unable to recognize her own son, her doctors said nothing more could be done and gave her six hours to live.*

Her daughter-in-law placed a photo of Sri Sri on her bed, held her hand, and prayed. The next day, to the amazement of all—especially the doctors—she could recognize everyone, and her blood sugar report, EEG, ECG, and all other reports were completely normal. She is now home and manages the house while her daughter-in-law completes TTC.

March 26, 1998
Lake Side; Chandigarh, India

146 Dreams

*W*HEN SOMETHING IS UNBELIEVABLY BEAUTIFUL OR joyful, you wonder if it is a dream. What you perceive as reality is often not joyful.

When misery is there you never wonder if it is a dream. You are sure it is real.

This is knowing the real as unreal, and unreal as real. In fact, all miseries are unreal. A wise man knows that happiness is real, a quality of your very nature. Unhappiness is unreal, as it is only an affliction of memory. When you can see both as a dream, then you abide in your true Self.

Payal: What about nightmares?

Sri Sri: A nightmare is mistaken as a reality only while you are dreaming.

Keep wondering whether your waking reality is a dream and you'll wake up to the real.

✎ News Flash

Rishikesh: The Advanced Course, Teacher Training, and Art Excel courses ended amidst jubilee. Many shared their healing experiences. The last few days, Satsang has been graced by saints from neighboring ashrams.

The trip from Rishikesh to Chandigarh was full of Sri Sri's mischief. The entourage stopped past midnight at Paonta Sahib, a Sikh holy shrine. The next evening, Satsang enraptured seven thousand.

April 2, 1998
Calcutta, India

147 Impression and Expression

*D*O NOT MAKE AN EFFORT TO IMPRESS OTHERS OR to express yourself.

Your effort to express yourself is an impediment. Your effort to impress someone becomes futile.

When you do not try to impress, expression comes naturally.
And when you come from the Self, your expression is perfect and your impression lasts for ages.

Often you don't seem to have control over your expressions—or the impressions you take in. Wisdom is selecting your expressions and impressions. Enlightenment is when impressions do not stay at all, whether good or bad. Nature has inbuilt in us a system which releases impressions through dreams and through meditation.

Many impressions in the mind cause:
- ▼ Confusion
- ▼ Distraction
- ▼ Chaos
- ▼ Lack of focus, and finally—
- ▼ Derangement of the mind.

Excessive expression makes you lose your depth, your luster, and the serenity of Self.

Meditation erases the impressions and gives you mastery of your expressions.

🕮 News Flash

Due to increasing crowds, Nitin and Bharat mentioned to Sri Sri that now he needs security guards. Watch out what you ask for in Guruji's presence! The next day, the government of Himachal Pradesh provided pilot cars and security for his entire trip in the Himalayan state.

Sri Sri had a whirlwind tour of Himachal Pradesh, with Satsangs in Kalka, Shimla, Nahan, Delhi, and NOIDA. Everyone marveled at Sri Sri's stamina and love.

From huge banners, TV screens—even movie theaters—Sri Sri smiled from every nook in Calcutta, the City of Joy, setting the stage for two grand Satsangs, where thousands are eagerly awaiting the Master.

April 9, 1998
Bangalore, India

148 Tarka, Vitarka, and Kutarka

To know yourself or to judge your actions, you need to know *tarka, vitarka* and *kutarka*.

Kutarka is wrong logic. For example: *The door is half open* means *the door is half closed;* therefore, *the door is fully open* means *the door is fully closed!*

Another example: *God is love; love is blind;* therefore, *God is blind!*

Many people misuse logic in this way and get caught up in ignorance.

Tarka is sequential logic; it increases scientific knowledge. But scientific conclusions change. For example: Pesticides were considered to be very useful in the past, but are now proven to be very harmful. With *tarka,* the paradigm changes in time.

Vitarka is asking questions which have no evident answers: "Who am I?" "What do I really want?" These philosophical questions increase your awareness and bring forth knowledge of the Self.

The wise know how to distinguish between these three.

News Flash

The Commissioner of Human Rights in Assam received Sri Sri in Guwahati.

The devotees trekked to a hilltop on the banks of the Brahmaputra River for a picnic with Sri Sri.

Guruji arrived the next day in Calcutta where the Ganguly home was enchantingly decorated in his honor.

Sri Sri addressed the Calcutta Management Association, and later enlightened ambassadors, officials, and politicians on Face to Face—*a television program.*

Eight thousand attended the Grand Satsang in Calcutta, where Sri Sri spoke little, but left everyone with happy smiles.

Sri Sri's black bag was lost—complete with passport and visas—but was found miraculously after a week.

Easter Advanced Courses are in progress all over the world.

April 15, 1998
German Academy

149 Softness and Forcefulness

*O*FTEN PEOPLE ARE SOFT FROM LACK OF COURAGE AND forcefulness. They suffer a lot, and at some time or other they become volatile.

Yet there are some people who possess a softness that comes from maturity, magnanimity, and the knowledge of the Self.

There are also two types of forcefulness in people: aggressive and assertive. Aggressive people are forceful out of weakness or out of fear. Assertive people are forceful out of care, love, and compassion.

David: Aggressive control and assertive support!

Sri Sri: So look into yourself and become aware of what type of softness and forcefulness you have.

✍ News Flash

Cherry blossoms and snow greeted Sri Sri at the German Academy.

Bulgaria, Namibia, and the Dominican Republic joined the Art of Living map this month.

April 22, 1998
Zen Monastery; Blois, France

150 Do Not Follow Me

Do not follow me. In fact, you cannot follow me, because I am behind you to push you forward!

You have to leave everything behind and move ahead. All your experiences, your relations—everything—is part of the past. Leave the whole world of your memories behind—including me. Drop everything. I am there behind you. Move on. Stop looking for more and be free! Then compassion will flow from you.

Question: When people do not follow anyone, isn't it usually out of fear or rebelliousness?

Sri Sri: One type of *Do not follow* comes from fear or rebelliousness. Another type comes from heightened awareness.

You cannot follow me because I am behind you and I am in you.
For long you have been a sheep.
Now it's time to be a lion.

✎ News Flash

Diplomats from various countries were touched to hear Sri Sri at an elegant event beautifully organized by Stella and her Geneva team.

Then began the whirlwind Tour de France...

Guruji and a bus load of gigglers traveled to five major French cities spreading waves of joy. The Master who lives in the present took us to the Futuroscope (a famous fun park). Guruji asked Denise, "Isn't this most beautiful?" Denise winked in reply, "It is only second."

In the car, Guruji gave the directions to the driver. Nathalie asked, "How can you know this place better than we do?" Guruji laughed and said, "I just guess!"

Opposite values are complementary; the lighthearted tour ended in a thought-provoking interfaith conference in Paris.

During the Weekly Knowledge meeting, Marcel asked, "How come I cannot follow the discussion sometimes?" Guruji said, "Well done!"

So, if you have not followed this Knowledge Sheet—well done!

April 29, 1998
Hamburg, Germany

151 Confusion and Decision

A DECISION IS REQUIRED ONLY WHEN THERE IS confusion. When there is no confusion, then there is no need of a decision.

If on your desk there is a piece of wood and a biscuit, you don't have to decide which to eat, do you? Decision is always about choice, and choice is always confusing. The more decisions, the more confused you are, swinging always between pain and pleasure. So, all decision-makers are confused! *(laughter)*

In you, there is an actor and there is a witness. An actor is either confused or decisive, but the witness just observes and smiles.

Action is spontaneous (no decision) when there is no actor. The more the witness grows in you, the more playful and untouched you are. Then trust, faith, love, and joy all manifest in and around you.

Are you confused, decisive, or happy now?

Eberhard: Confusion is too strong of an expression. Is it not rather that we need to make a choice?

Urmila: We are decided that choice is confusion. *(everyone laughs)*

Hans Peter: Is there any freedom without confusion?

Sri Sri: When you are confused, there is no freedom.

Hans Peter: Then what is freedom of choice?

Sri Sri: Confusion! *(laughter)*

✍ News Flash

There was a big discussion about whether Guruji should wear a plain white shawl or a white shawl with gold for the evening Human Values Conference. This choice confused everyone, but provided lots of laughter!

May 6, 1998
Rome, Italy

152 You are Privileged

*A*MONG ALL THE PLANETS IN OUR SOLAR SYSTEM, the earth is privileged to host life in so many forms.

Among all the species, humans are most privileged, for they can host the Knowledge.

Among all the knowledgeable ones, you are the most privileged...guess why?

The underprivileged are those who do not realize that they are privileged. They also host, but they host all the negativities.

Again and again, remember that you are peace, you are love, you are joy, and that you host the Creator. If you don't realize you are the host, you live like a ghost.

Like the birds returning to their nests, again and again come back to your Source; only there can you realize that you host the Divine.

News Flash

A happy crowd greeted Sri Sri with loud applause after a debate and short meditation at the Inter-Faith Conference on Human Values, held in the prestigious Hamburg University Auditorium.

The Indian Ambassador in Vienna hosted a Satsang at his gracious home.

Sri Sri and his ideas delighted nearly 150 diplomats and U.N. officials at a meeting organized by Mary and her team in Vienna.

May 6 marks Sri Sri's first visit to Rome in eleven years.

May 14, 1998
Bangalore Ashram, India

153 The Value of Chanting

When you sing bhajans, the vibration of sound energy gets absorbed into every atom of your body. This enkindles the energy in you and brings up the consciousness. Your entire body gets soaked in energy. Transformation happens.

A microphone absorbs sound and converts it into electricity; the body absorbs sound vibration and converts it into consciousness.

If you sit and listen to gossip or violent music, then that energy gets absorbed by your body and does not give a nice feeling.

When you hear the Knowledge or chant with all your heart, that elevates your consciousness.

An ancient proverb in Sanskrit says that the words of rishis and enlightened ones are translated into experience immediately.

Bawa: We have read and heard from so many people, but when Guruji speaks the same knowledge, it straightaway hits home.

🖉 News Flash

A family of devotees found, within a few weeks of doing Sudarshan Kriya, that their cat—whose diet had been exclusively dried fish—has turned vegetarian and will not even look at fish anymore!

One of our teachers had an operation, and later discovered that the absent-minded surgeon had left a metal clip inside her abdomen. In addition, a large stone developed in the gall bladder which caused an internal abscess. She had planned to go to the Bangalore Ashram, but instead had to be scheduled for surgery on the day of her intended departure. Upon examination, the doctors were surprised to discover that there was no clip, no stone—and no abscess!

Sri Sri was not born, but 2000 people came to the Bangalore Ashram to celebrate his birthday. Everyone applauded Prashanth and his housing team for the way they avoided chaos.

P.S. Ishani and Bawa's dogs also turned vegetarian.

May 21, 1998
Bangalore Ashram, India

154 Intensify Your Longing

Attainment of the Divine depends on the intensity of longing and not on the time or qualification.

A proverb among the villagers in India says, "It may take some time to pluck a flower, but it takes no time to meet the Divine!" Your abilities or qualifications are not the criteria—it is simply the intensity of your longing.

Intensify your longing for the Divine right away. This happens when you know that you are nothing and that you want nothing.

Suneeta: If we are nothing and we want nothing, then how can longing come?

Sidappa: Knowing you are nothing and you want nothing brings belongingness...

Sri Sri: ...and belongingness intensifies longing.

Bill: What is the difference between desire and longing?

Sri Sri:

Desire is the fever of the head.
Longing is the cry of the heart.

✎ **News Flash**

The Ashram is buzzing with Advanced Courses, the Indian Teachers Meeting, Teacher Training, and Art Excel! Housing has overflowed into neighboring resorts and hostels. Huge tents were pitched for meditation. Everyone felt a dire need for a bigger meditation hall and dining room.

Even with this shortage, Sri Sri came up with yet another seva project: Health, Hygiene, Home, and Human values—the four H's. In less than an hour, inspired devotees took up seva projects to provide drinking water, sanitary facilities, prayer halls, and over 600 homes for the homeless in rural districts all over India.

Vikram: Someone should take up a similar project for the Ashram!

May 28, 1998
Bangalore Ashram, India

155 Faith is Your Wealth

*I*F YOU THINK YOUR FAITH IN GOD IS DOING A FAVOR to *God,* then you are mistaken. Your faith in God or Guru does nothing to God or Guru. Faith is *your* wealth.

Faith gives you strength instantly. Faith brings you stability, centeredness, calmness, and love. Faith is your blessing.

If you lack faith, you will have to pray for faith. But to pray, you need faith. This is a paradox. *(Laughter)*

People put their faith in the world, but the whole world is just a soap bubble. People have faith in themselves, but they don't know who they are. People think that they have faith in God, but they really do not know who God is.

There are three types of faith:

1) Faith in yourself: Without faith in yourself, you think *I can't do this; This is not for me; I will never be liberated in this life.*

2) Faith in the world: You must have faith in the world or you can't move an inch. You deposit money in the bank with faith that it will be returned. If you doubt everything, nothing will happen for you.

3) Faith in the Divine: Have faith in the Divine and you will evolve.

All these faiths are connected; you must have all three for each to be strong. If you start doubting in one, you will begin to doubt everything.

Bill: Atheists have faith in themselves and faith in the world, but not in God.
Sri Sri: Then they don't have complete faith in themselves. And their faith in the world cannot be constant because there are always changes. Lack of faith in God, the world, or yourself brings fear.
Faith makes you full—faithful.

Rajesh: What's the difference between faith and confidence?
Sri Sri: Faith is the beginning. Confidence is the result. Faith in yourself brings freedom. Faith in the world brings you peace of mind. Faith in God evokes love in you.

Having faith in the world without faith in God does not bring complete peace. But if you have love, you automatically have peace and freedom. People who are extremely disturbed should only have faith in God.

News Flash

During a late afternoon Satsang at Sumeru Mantap, Sri Sri started chanting. Suddenly, people started pointing to a huge thundercloud in the western sky filled with brilliant colors of unusual intensity. The trees had been crying for water, and within a few minutes, the wind came up and a delicious rain began to fall. But what were these colors? It was not a rainbow. We contacted the weather observatory, but they had no idea of this phenomenon. When we asked Guruji for an explanation, he replied, "Nature is our friend."

After hectic activities in Bangalore, Guruji tried to escape to Mangalore for 24 hours, but it turned into another party!

Art of Living representatives, headed by Sharada Lavingia, were invited to the G-8 Summit reception in Birmingham, U.K.

Art of Living was also represented in the World Health Organization Conference in Geneva, Switzerland.

Teachers presented programs in St. Petersburg, Russia.

Women's prison programs have started in Bangalore.

Reports of more seva projects are arriving from all over the world.

June 3, 1998
Curepipe, Mauritius

156 Who Wakes Up First?

WHO WAKES UP FIRST—YOU OR GOD?
YOU wake up first—while God is still asleep!
When you wake up, you experience pleasure and pain. You become aware of the beauty and the shortcomings of the world. Then, when you seek the ultimate, your cry for help wakes up God. And when God is awakened in you, there is no "two."

God is asleep in every particle of this universe. God is in you in seed form. When he wakes up, neither you nor the world remain.

The rishis made a mock practice of awakening God every morning. They call it *Suprabhatam* service. Many people find this ridiculous because they don't understand the depth of it. Only awakened God can see that God is everywhere asleep! *(laughter)*

Brenda: Why should we wake up?
Sri Sri: Because you are not asleep. If you are asleep, how can you ask the question?
Bill: Once you are awake, can you go back to sleep?
Sri Sri: If you have not had tea, of course.
Bill: Who wakes us up?
Sri Sri: You figure that out.

News Flash

A tree-planting program has taken root at the Bangalore Ashram.

Sri Sri met with local people, inaugurated the 4-H program (Health, Hygiene, Home, and Human values), and initiated Satsang groups in the villages around the Ashram.

Bombay was plastered with big billboards that attracted over 5000 to the Satsang. Arriving at the airport for the trip to Mauritius, Guruji and entourage were told the flight was overbooked. Sri Sri showed his "Guru Card" and suddenly all seven travelers had seats.

Mauritius hosted many events: interviews with television and radio, two Satsangs, a lecture at the University, audiences with the President and Prime Minister, a meeting with wardens and other prison officials, and, as part of a local seva project which the Art of Living organization has adopted—a visit to an old-age home (which is where you may be by the end of this sentence).

Vikram recorded Seeds of Wisdom at a local radio station, which will broadcast one quote each day over the next month.

This completes the third year of Weekly Knowledge.

Homework for next week: Everyone write a Weekly Knowledge sheet.

June 10, 1998
New York, New York

157 Breaking Beyond the Rational Mind

*Y*OU USUALLY DO ONLY THAT WHICH IS PURPOSEFUL, useful, and rational. Everything you see, you see through the rational mind.

But an intuition, a discovery, a new knowledge goes beyond the rational mind. Truth is beyond reason.

The rational mind is like a railroad track that is fixed in grooves. Truth needs no tracks. Truth can float anywhere like a balloon.

Some people step out of the rational mind in order to rebel against society. They want to break social law, but it is for the sake of ego—out of anger, hatred, rebelliousness, and wanting attention. This is not stepping out of the rational mind (though they may think it is).

We step out of the rational mind when we do something that has no purpose. If there is no purpose, the action becomes a game. Life becomes lighter.

If you are stuck with only rational acts, life is a burden. But if you play a game without a thought of winning or losing, if you do something without any purpose attached to it—just act irrationally—it is freedom, like a dance.

Just step out of the rational mind and you'll find a great freedom, an unfathomable depth, and you'll come face-to-face with reality.

Reality transcends logic and the rational mind. Until you transcend the rational mind, you will not get access to creativity and the Infinite.

But remember: if you do an irrational act in order to find freedom, then you already have a purpose. It is no longer irrational. This Weekly Knowledge note has already spoiled its own possibility!

Break the barrier of the rational mind and find freedom for yourself.

News Flash

That old Guru Magic worked so well and got Botswana and South Africa in its spell. Sri Sri's talk made headline news in Johannesburg and Durban.

Senior government officials and prominent religious leaders met Sri Sri at our International Symposium on Human Values. The Premier of the Kwa-Zulu Natal Province offered to organize courses in the local prisons. Our International Association for Human Values 1998 Award was given to President Nelson Mandela. The African tour left crowds reeling.

Sri Sri moved on to crowds in Atlanta and New York, and tomorrow he will address the Values Caucus at the United Nations.

June 17, 1998
Baltimore, Maryland

158 If You Cannot Meditate —Be Stupid!

*I*F YOU ARE UNABLE TO MEDITATE, IF YOUR MIND IS chattering too much and nothing works, just feel that you are a little stupid. Then you will be able to sink deep.

Your intellect is a small portion of your total consciousness. If you are stuck in the intellect, you miss a lot.

Happiness is when you transcend the intellect. When you feel stupid or in awe, you transcend the intellect.

Have you noticed how mentally retarded people are more happy?

Question: How do you go beyond the intellect?
Sri Sri: By acting stupid! Everyone avoids being stupid —no one wants to look dumb. That is really stupid.

Stupidity should be followed by meditation, otherwise depression may follow.

Question: Can I ask a stupid question?
Sri Sri: All questions are anyway stupid.
Mikey: How do you become stupid?
Yash: By asking the question.
Rajshree: Just be yourself!

✎ News Flash

Torrential rains hit New England as Sri Sri and his entourage gave talks in Boston. The mayor declared a state of emergency. Many true seekers traveled for hours through the storms and, miraculously, the rain stopped for three hours while Guruji gave a Satsang.

Sri Sri attended the Baltimore conference on Breaking the Cycle of Violence. Dr. Ganesh Prabhu, Tom Duffy, Odyl Wittman, and Ronnie Newman gave presentations on the health benefits of Sudarshan Kriya and the Prison Smart Program—including the women's program and groundbreaking independent research on juvenile offenders. Our panel stirred up a storm of interest with the enthusiastic audience.

June 24, 1998
St. Louis, Missouri

159 Give Away Your Rights

*T*HOSE WHO FIGHT FOR THEIR RIGHTS ARE WEAK; they do not know their inner strength, their magnanimity.

The weaker you are, the more you demand your rights. Asserting your rights makes you isolated and poor. People take pride in fighting for their rights. This is an ignorant pride. You need to recognize that no one can take away your rights: they are yours.

Courageous people give away their rights. The degree to which you give away your rights indicates your freedom, your strength. Only those who have rights can give them away!

Demanding rights does not really bring rights to you, and giving away rights does not really take them away.

Poor are those who demand rights. Richer are those who know that their rights cannot be taken away. Richest are those who give away their rights.

Demand for rights is ignorance, agony.
Knowing that no one can take away your rights is freedom.
Giving away your rights is love, wisdom.

✎ **News Flash**

Heavy cyclones hit the coastal areas of Gujarat, India. More than a thousand people were killed; five thousand are missing. Art of Living chapters sent teams of volunteers with ten tons of grain, ten thousand garments, and medicines to the villages of the Jamnagar District—the hardest hit. Volunteers raised a fund of 250,000 rupees in just two days.

Four successful courses for women prisoners in Bangalore reported miraculous experiences. Cases of hernia, asthma, and appendicitis were completely cured. Participants reported visions of Sri Sri.

Veena Gandhi, a relative of Mahatma Gandhi, hosted a Satsang in Philadelphia.

In Pittsburgh, Sri Sri enjoyed a university professor who attempted to disrupt the meeting, but whose heckling only added charm.

July 1, 1998
Vancouver, Canada

160 Generosity is a Quality of Spirit

WHEN YOU FEEL STUCK IN LIFE—NOT GROWING, bombarded by desires, dry, lacking enthusiasm, no juice —what do you do?

Here is the solution:

FEEL GENEROUS...right away, not tomorrow.

Generosity is a quality of spirit. A prince or a pauper can both feel generous. When you feel generous, your life becomes abundant, full of compassion and love.

Question: Is generosity the same as being grateful?
Sri Sri: No, gratefulness always has self-concern. Why are you grateful? Because you have something or you will get something.

Generosity is independent of external circumstances. No one else can make you feel generous. It is something you have to do by yourself. Generosity is a state of consciousness. Generosity is not an act, but it always finds its expression in an act.

Question: What about passion?
Sri Sri: Passion indicates scarcity; dispassion is abun-

dance. But dispassion without generosity makes you self-centered and causes dryness.

Don't think about what you've done in the past; that only brings doership. Just feel generous.

News Flash
A successful prison program is now in progress following Sri Sri's visit to South Africa (see Weekly Knowledge #157).

Sri Sri came to Chicago for inspiring talks and intimate Satsangs. As the Knowledge flowed, each devotee felt Guruji was speaking personally to them.

In Jackson Hole, Wyoming, the weather was cool while the volunteers were hot arranging packed talks.

In Vancouver, Guruji was again met by sunshine—in the sky and on the faces of devotees.

July 9, 1998
Lake Tahoe, California

161 The Path of Love is Surrender

*K*RISHNA FIRST TELLS ARJUNA, "YOU ARE VERY dear to me." Then Krishna tells Arjuna he must surrender.

Surrender begins with an assumption. First you must assume you are the most beloved of the Divine; then surrender happens.

Surrender is not an action, it is an assumption. Non-surrender is ignorance, an illusion.

Surrender has to begin as an assumption and then it reveals itself as a reality. And finally, it reveals itself as an illusion, because there is no "two"—no duality.

No one has any independent existence! That is it!

Question: Do you have to go through surrender to realize surrender is an illusion?

Sri Sri: Yes, absolutely.

Question: Where is choice then?

Sri Sri: The choice is your destiny. Krishna doesn't tell Arjuna in the beginning that he must surrender. First he says, "You are so dear to me." Later he tells him, "There is no other choice for you—you must surrender. Either do it now, or you will do it later."

This is the path of love.

✎ **News Flash**

Hundreds of grateful devotees greeted Guruji under a full Guru Purnima moon at beautiful Lake Tahoe. During the evening celebration, devotees floated across the stage for blessings from Sri Sri to the sweet chant of Om Namo Bhagavate. *A huge brown mama bear and her cub came out of the mountains to join the festivities.*

July 15, 1998
Alpine Meadows, California

162 It Takes Courage to Say "I Am"

The Divine comes only in deep rest—not by *doing*.

All your spiritual doings are to help you become silent. You will go further when you do not stop to enjoy the bliss or the peace, otherwise cravings may arise.

If existence wants to give you peace and bliss, then fine; your true nature is bliss. But by trying to enjoy the bliss, you step down from "am-ness" to "I am *something*"— "I am peaceful," "I am blissful"—and this is followed by, "I am miserable." It takes courage to simply say "I am"— *period*. "I am" is dispassion.

Dispassion means welcoming everything. You can be anywhere and be dispassionate. Dispassionate centeredness brings energy, a spark. Indulgence in bliss brings inertia.

If you are dispassionate, the bliss is still there. When the freezer is full of ice cream, you need not bother about it.

Dispassion takes away a sense of scarcity. Passion is a sense of lack of abundance.

Whenever everything is in abundance, dispassion happens.
And when dispassion is there, everything comes in abundance.

Question: What do we do when we catch ourselves indulging in bliss?

Sri Sri: Just this understanding creates a shift. There is no effort. Knowledge is better than action to make you free.

✍ News Flash

Under crystal skies, surrounded by the snow-capped mountains of Alpine Meadows, the week-long gathering included an Advanced Course, a weekend and six-day Basic Course, Teacher Training 1-3, Parenting the Angels, and ART Excel. The teenagers kidnapped Sri Sri for an afternoon of ice-skating and laughter.

July 23, 1998
Denver, Colorado

163 Do You Know I Have No Mercy?

MERCY INDICATES LACK OF INTIMACY—A distance, a lack of belonging.

You don't have mercy on your near and dear ones. You don't hear parents say, "I have mercy on my children."

You have mercy only on those whom you think are not yours. Mercy indicates anger, judgment and authority.

When you ask for mercy, you are self-centered. You want to be excused from the law of cause and effect. It indicates lack of courage and valor.

At times, mercy is an impediment to growth. Mercy, of course, brings some comfort and relief, but can impair a transformation. If the leaves were to ask for mercy from falling, what would happen to the tree?

Patti and Victoria, high on bliss, did not stop at a stop sign, so the police mercilessly gave them a ticket. Victoria said, "Thank you," but the police woman told her to go to court and beg for mercy! *(laughter)*

When you know and trust the process of creation, you will simply rejoice.

You only ask for mercy if you think that God is angry and judging you. This is the small mind superimposing itself on the Divine mind. The Divine is all-knowing and all-loving—there is no chance for mercy.

Do you know I have no mercy? There is intimacy here and no place for mercy.

Sri Sri
Jai Guru Dev

✍ News Flash

The summer tour continued in the San Francisco Bay area and Santa Cruz, where sold-out talks swept away the crowds with knowledge and grace.

Sri Sri visited the infamous "Mystery Spot" and, of course, solved the mysteries.

Record-high temperatures and record-high bliss followed the entourage to three Colorado cities for standing-room-only crowds and joyous Satsangs.

The **Art of Living Foundation** is devoted to making your life a celebration. A nonprofit educational organization run entirely by volunteers, we offer workshops for self-development and spiritual growth that allow busy people to take maximum advantage of Sri Sri's multidimensional teachings. We are officially accredited as an NGO with the United Nations, and we sponsor service projects worldwide, including programs for people living with HIV and cancer, rehabilitative training for prisoners, and vocational training for rural people in Asia. Our "Dollar-a-Day" program provides children with food, clothing, and schooling.

▲ You can visit our web site on the Internet at: **www.artofliving.org**

▲ **The Art of Living Basic Course—Grace Through the Breath** is the ideal introduction to Sri Sri's wisdom. This 16-18 hour program over 4-6 days has uplifted the lives of thousands.

Breath contains the secret of life. Breath is linked to the vital energy in us, or *prana*. Low prana translates into depression, lethargy, dullness, and poor enthusiasm. When mind and body are charged with prana, we feel alert, energetic, and full of good humor. Specific breathing techniques can revitalize our prana and invigorate our physical and emotional well-being. You will learn several potent breathing practices, including *Sudarshan Kriya*, a unique practice that fully oxygenates the cells, recharging them with new energy and life. Negative emotions—stored as toxins in the body—are easily uprooted and flushed out. Tension, frustration, and anger get released. Anxiety, depression, and lethargy are washed away. The mind is left calm and centered, with a clearer vision of the world, our relationships, and ourselves. The heart of the workshop also includes processes and precious insights into the nature of life and how to be happy. To take this workshop, contact the Art of Living Center nearest you *(see directory, page 119)*.

▲ **Art of Living Advanced Courses** are specially designed for those who have completed the Basic Course. These in-residence retreats provide you a profound opportunity to explore the depths of your own inner silence through deep meditation. Various games and enjoyable processes keep everybody guessing what will come next. Each evening ends with a celebration of singing, dancing, and marvelous wisdom. You leave feeling renewed emotionally and elevated spiritually, with a dynamic freshness for greater success in all your activities.

Some Advanced Courses are offered in Sri Sri's presence—and meeting the Master personally is the experience of a lifetime...

▲ **Sahaj Samadhi Meditation**
Not one of us lacks spiritual depth. The peace and happiness we feverishly seek in the world are already contained within us, covered only by the clouds of stress and strain. These clouds are lifted with Sahaj Samadhi meditation—a gift of wisdom from Sri Sri.

Sahaj Samadhi meditation provides a rest much deeper than sleep. Like awakening renewed on a sunny morning, your outlook on life becomes realigned towards the positive. Stress drops off, the chattering mind becomes serene and creative, aging slows, and you rediscover the unshakable contentment of your inner Self. Sahaj Samadhi meditation is easy to learn and practice. With simple guidance, anyone can meditate. Personal instruction is offered at Art of Living Centers worldwide.

▲ **Books, videos, and audiotapes of Sri Sri** are available by mail. Titles include: *The Way of Grace, The Meaning of Life, The Nature of Enlightenment, Om Shanti, The Path of Love, Peace is Our Nature, What is a Guru?,* and the *Yoga Sutras of Patanjali.*

For a catalog, please call or write:

Art of Living Books and Tapes
P.O. Box 50003, Santa Barbara, CA 93150
Toll Free: (800) 574-3001; Outside USA: (805) 563-6396

▲ **ART OF LIVING CENTERS WORLDWIDE:**

UNITED STATES: Art of Living General Information (800) 897-5913 or (805) 563-6396; **ARIZONA** Phoenix (520) 284-5330; Sedona (520) 284-5330; **CALIFORNIA** Laguna Beach (714) 494-5746; Los Angeles (310) 820-9429; Oakland (510) 530-5464; Orange County (949) 493-4574; Monterey (831) 372-1803; Mountain View (650) 969-6611; San Diego (619) 581-9011; San Jose (415) 964-8908; Santa Barbara (805) 565-3603; Santa Rosa (707) 887-7720; **COLORADO** Boulder (303) 652-8294; Cascade (719) 684-8003; Colorado Springs (719) 488-9478; Denver (303) 333-3031; **CONNECTICUT** Woodbridge (203) 397-0510; **D.C.** (202) 526-5961; **FLORIDA** Miami/Ft. Lauderdale (954) 721-7437; Orlando (407) 321-2527; Punta Gorda (941) 575-2617; St. Petersburg (813) 521-2787; Tampa (813) 888-9912; Venice (813) 497-5474; **GEORGIA** Atlanta (770) 937-9323; **HAWAII** Kauaʻi (808) 826-5595; Oahu (808) 944-3323; **ILLINOIS** Chicago (847) 604-1452; **IOWA** Fairfield (515) 472-2053; **MARYLAND** Baltimore (410) 527-0768; Bowie (301) 464-8092; Clarksville (301) 854-0087; Greenbelt (301) 552-0060; Silver Spring (301) 588-6422, (301) 585-9126; **MASSACHUSETTS** Boston (617) 354-5566; Cape Cod (508) 349-3591; **MICHIGAN**

Detroit (810) 790-2875; Flint (810) 736-2966; **MINNESOTA** Minneapolis (612) 786-1688; **MISSOURI** Kansas City (800) 446-1746; Kirksville (816) 665-3004; St. Louis (314) 207-0922; **MONTANA** Bozeman (406) 586-7181; **NEVADA** Lake Tahoe (702)-721-5879; Las Vegas (702) 897-9177; **NEW JERSEY** Somerset (732) 855-5277; **NEW MEXICO** Albuquerque (505) 898-3306; Grants (505) 876-2564; Santa Fe (505) 984-0327; **NEW YORK** Ithaca (607) 533-8710; La Grangeville (914) 677-5871; Manhattan (212) 353-9252; **NORTH CAROLINA** Raleigh (919) 785-2200; **OHIO** Cincinnati (513) 321-1049; Cleveland (216) 243-7427; **OREGON** Portland (503) 675-1778; Washougal (360) 835-0731; **PENNSYLVANIA** Philadelphia (215) 247-3305; Pittsburgh (412) 367-4688; **TEXAS** Dallas (972) 517-2213; Houston (281) 564-2216; San Antonio (830) 537-4875; **VIRGINIA** (703) 644-1615; **WASHINGTON** Redmond (425) 868-2561; Seattle (206) 328-0122; Sequim (360) 582-0346; **WYOMING** Jackson (307) 734-1880; **INTERNATIONAL CENTERS: AUSTRALIA** (61) 26 287-4004; **AZERBAIDZHAN** Baku 994-12-98-73-25; **BELORUSSIA** (CIS) +375-17-2304265; **BOTSWANA** (267) 352175; **CANADA** (819) 532-3328; Calgary (403) 289-6500; Montreal (514) 670-5728; Nova Scotia (902) 835-6016; Toronto (416) 960-0376; Vancouver (604) 228-8728; **COLUMBIA** (571) 619-2309; **COSTA RICA** 78-2501; **CROATIA** Buje 385-52-773505; **KOPRIVNICA** 385-43-827-157; **CZECH REPUBLIC** 42-2-27-1611; **DENMARK** 45-33-323545; **ENGLAND** (44) 181-747-9494; **FINLAND** 358 41 607081; **FRANCE** 33-5490-28543; **GERMANY** 49-7804-910923; **HONG KONG** (852) 2337-6696; **INDIA** (91) 80-6645-106; **INDONESIA** (62) 21 651 3123; **ITALY** Florence 39-55-4491631; Milano 39 0226144598 **IVORY COAST** (225) 43 2569; **JAPAN** 03-3328-5392; **LITHUANIA** 370-33-55541; **MALAYSIA** (03) 442-2070; **MAURITIUS** (230) 6764557; **NEPAL** (1) 523360; **NETHERLANDS** 31-72-5152240; **NORWAY** 47-22-364083; **PANAMA** 194-4645 & 233-3479; **POLAND** 48-22-6437544; **RUSSIA** Moscow 7-095-978-8626; Irkutsk (3952) 53054, Krasnoyarsk (3912) 49-85-31; **ST. LUCIA** 758-452-8268; **SINGAPORE** (65) 337-2341; **SLOVENIA** 386-61-343992; **SOUTH AFRICA** (011) 839-1255; **SWEDEN** 46-8-30 70 04; **SWITZERLAND** 41-22-7000114; **TAIWAN** R.O.C. (886) 2-881-2882; **TRINIDAD** 868-645-5268; **U.A.E.** 971-2-327507